Jesus

Nicholas Michael Battiston

AuthorHouse™
1663 Liberty Drive
Bloomington, IN 47403
www.authorhouse.com
Phone: 1 (800) 839-8640

Scripture taken from the New King James Version. Copyright 1982 by Thomas Nelson, Inc.
Used by permission. All rights reserved.

Published by AuthorHouse 06/04/2019

ISBN: 978-1-4520-9493-9 (sc)
ISBN: 978-1-7283-1575-1 (e)

Library of Congress Control Number: 2011913598

Print information available on the last page.

authorHOUSE®

Contents

CHAPTER 1:

My Story

I began my relationship with Jesus when I got sick and wasn't healing. I turned to the Lord after realizing that I wasn't getting any better. I started watching the preachers on TV, reading the Bible, and completing curriculum based on God's word.

Chapter 2:
Revelations

God has taught me to help others. God has taught me that I am healed by Jesus's stripes.

1 Peter 2:24

who Himself bore our sins in His own body on the tree, that we, having died to sins, might live for righteousness—by whose stripes you were healed.

The passage below really struck me because this made me realize that by not helping the poor I was in fact not respecting life, I was not respecting people, and I was not helping God and his kingdom.

Matthew 25:40

And the King will answer and say to them, "Assuredly, I say to you, in as much as you did *it* to one of the least of these My brethren, you did *it* to Me."

CHAPTER 3:

Passions

God has shaped me to care most about furthering the gospel, helping the poor, helping those who are being used as sexual slaves, and the environment. The way that I show God that these issues are important to me is to give my money to organizations that are helping the sexually exploited. I also volunteer to help the homeless. I have eliminated paper and gone paperless where I can, I pick up garbage, and I carefully watch my carbon footprint.

CHAPTER 4:

The good news is that God is no respecter of persons; what he does for one group of people he will do for all—not by might but by his spirit.God offers salvation to those who accept Jesus as their personal Lord and savior and believe in Him. Jesus says to Nicodemus that one must be born again to see the kingdom of heaven.The Holy Spirit has shown me that being born again is realizing I can't do it on my own—seeing that I need the Lord, I need Christ.Seeing the way you were prior to being born again for me was seeing that I was selfish and self-centered and then coming to the realization that I needed Jesus.

John 3:3

Jesus answered and said to him, "Most assuredly, I say to you, unless one is born again, he cannot see the kingdom of God."

CHAPTER 5:

Jesus

Before I met Jesus my life was programmed by what I saw on the Internet and in the mainstream media.Before I met Jesus I was always looking to myself to accomplish goals, make financial decisions, and guide my life, and much of these decisions ended in loss.

Prior to meeting Jesus my life was fast paced, but I was on a fast track to nowhere, with no guarantee of heaven.

CHAPTER 6:

Who?

I realized I needed Jesus when everything else I was doing wasn't working. The medications weren't working, self-help books were not working, and everything I was trying wasn't working.

CHAPTER 7:

How?

I committed my life to Jesus by

- accepting him as my Lord and savior;
- giving money to various organizations, charities, and ministries;
- volunteering my time to help the homeless and to spreading the gospel to the world;
- telling my family and friends about Jesus;
- reading the Bible;
- studying God's word; and
- completing a curriculum that teaches God's word.

CHAPTER 8:

Change

Jesus has done so much for me. Jesus has relieved me of stress and saved me from going to hell. Jesus has given me a purpose, which is to help others. Jesus has made my life bear fruit.

CHAPTER 9:

Teachings

- God has taught me, from failure, that great change can come after failure.
- God has taught me, from lack of money, that you can still give even when you have little and give with a merry heart even with a lack of money.Even when you can only give on credit cards, you can still give and trust the Lord.
- God has taught me, from pain and sorrow, that Jesus died for my sins and bore my sicknesses on the tree, that I am healed by Jesus's stripes,and that because of this I should not be sick.
- God has taught me, through waiting, that good things will come to those who wait patiently and stay in the word, just as good has come to me.
- God has taught me, through illness, that at the end of the illness you can come out as a much stronger person and that God can turn what Satan tried to steal into triumph.
- God has taught me, through disappointment,that I should give my concern regarding my disappointment to him because he cares for me.

1 Peter 5:7

… casting all your care upon Him, for He cares for you.

- I learned, from my family, to listen to your family even if you are not sure what they mean at first because Jesus can show you what they mean.
- I have learned, from other Christians, to stay in the word and to help others and give money towards furthering the gospel.
- I have learned, from my relationships, to be strong and love the Lord.
- From my small group I have learned to love them, even when they don't have the same views as I do.
- I have learned, from my critics' contemplation, analyzing what I say and what I think, to align with how I truly feel in accordance with the word of God.

CHAPTER 10

Nicholas's 14 Steps to Total Victory

1. Watch the preachers on television; pick a few that you like.
2. Read the Bible and memorize scriptures.
3. Volunteer.
4. Don't suck in your stomach or hold up your shoulders; if you don't like how your body looks, you can exercise. Also, if you don't like your face, don't try to change it by puckering your lips or squinting your eyes. You should pray to God about this; your bones will hold you up.I did this and stopped doing it.
5. Speak the word from your heart—don't be afraid.
6. Give 10 percent of your gross income to increase and further God's kingdom.
7. Study a curriculum that teaches the Bible.
8. Partner up with the preachers on television.
9. Help the poor and the sexually exploited.
10. Help the widows and orphans.
11. Pray for yourself and pray for others.In prayer, ask for the Holy Spirit to help you and ask your Father in the third heaven for help.
12. Fast.

Matthew 17:20–21

So Jesus said to them, "Because of your unbelief; for assuredly, I say to you, if you have faith as a mustard seed, you will say to this mountain, 'Move from here to there,' and it will move; and nothing will be impossible for you. However, this kind does not go out except by prayer and fasting."

13. Separate what you think, what people think, and what God thinks.
14. Always remember that people have opinions, but that doesn't mean they are right; likewise, just because you may have an opinion doesn't mean you are right.

CHAPTER II:
Miracles

Healed of Sleep Apnea
Healed of Bipolar Affective Disorder
Off all medication
I can rhyme and act after reading the Bible
Able to read books better
Able to volunteer
Freedom from fear
Able to complete home hardware projects
Wrote this book

Acts 15:12

Then all the multitude kept silent and listened to Barnabas and Paul declaring how many miracles and wonders God had worked through them among the Gentiles.

Printed in the United States
By Bookmasters